All photos were taken in Wheathampstead in 2018 by Susan L'Estrange, unless they clearly weren't.
(OK, a few were taken by Hugh L'Estrange who is also responsible for the clever shopping of photos.)
All were taken in places accessible to the public.
However things change, and life moves on – as it should –
so there is no guarantee that all the things depicted in these exact pictures could be found again.
But that's not the point.
As you look for these – and for similar things, and for all the things which weren't there
to be photographed for this book – you'll find your own whimsical whonders.
Enjoy them.

Some of the most important skills for young (and older) people to acquire in today's fast-changing world
are curiosity, creativity and the ability to discern the difference between fake news and truth.
This book is offered as an opportunity for you to practise.

WWW*

is about looking and seeing – and maybe seeing things a little bit differently.
It's also supposed to be fun, so please don't take it **too** seriously.

* Pity we didn't think to trademark 'www'!

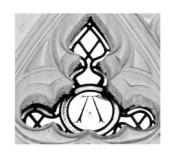

"*The real voyage of discovery consists
not in seeking new landscapes,
but in having new eyes*"

Marcel Proust

CONTENTS and malcontents

ANSWERS

The aim of this book is to encourage you to go out and about in Wheathampstead, to see new things (or things anew) and look for answers for yourself – but if you really can't find them (in the book or in the village), some help (but only some) is given at the bottom of pages and on pages 46-47.

Whonderful Whimsical Wheathampstead
is dedicated to the whonderful young people in our lives
– particularly grandsons and nephews
Michael, Thomas, Toby, George, Jonathan, Harry and Rafael –
and to the Wheathampstead community who have made us so whelcome

Whelcome to Wheathamstead

Those of us who have the privilege of living in Wheathampstead know that it is a truly splendid village. Although many of the things you can see here can also be found elsewhere, in many respects this village is unique. Or maybe it depends on how you look at things.

We are well-endowed with gardens, playgrounds, parks and green spaces, which can look like this ...

... or this

In some respects the village is quite old fashioned ...

... we still work in old money

(How much is 40 shillings?)

... and old telephone numbers

... and we honestly do measure our allotments in poles!
But we're forward-looking in our attempts to contact aliens

We're the home of the original Ash Grove – about which the song was written (the one that goes da da da, da-da da da, da da da-da-da-da da da ...)

... and fiercely protective of our potato copyright

We're very patriotic ...

... and generous.

Village centre
P Free

However ... there are some no-go areas

DANGER OF DEATH

... watch out for dare-devil motorbike riders

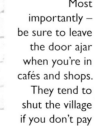

... and we aren't equally welcoming to everyone.

HIPPIES USE SIDE DOOR

Most importantly – be sure to leave the door ajar when you're in cafés and shops. They tend to shut the village if you don't pay attention.

Sorry WE'RE CLOSED

Give us a sign

Wheathampstead is truly a village full of wonder. It has its own microclimate as well as the potential to have different weather conditions at different parts of the village, and also different seasons and different times of day – all at once. But there are six signs leading into Wheathampstead. Which one is missing here?

SPRING

Wheathampstead in the rain

Wheathampstead is quite a big place and it's not quite clear where it begins and ends – the village and parish boundaries seem to be different.
But most things mentioned in this book can be found around the centre – the area you'll find on the numerous Heritage Maps. And do look at the maps – they're all different and a great source of information.

AUTUMN

Wheathampstead at night

Wheathampstead in the fog

SUMMER

WINTER

You'll find at least six ways into the village – but please note there is **NO WAY OUT!**

To P or not to P – that is the question

There has been some controversy over the spelling of the name of the village and you used to find two different forms prominently displayed. However, after the demonstrations during the 'p-ing war' of 2018, the Parish Council voted unanimously to 'keep the ps'. Most people comply – although you do see occasional rogue variations (look out for 'Wheath'std' in St Albans).

SAVE OUR P

P 4 WHEATHAMPSTEAD

WE WANT A P

A controversial full stop (see page 40) and a scuzzy road sign!

Early forms of the name were **Whethamstede** and **Hwaethamstede** (the latter was presumably the preference of people who liked to say 'hwich' and 'hwere' rather than 'which' and 'where'). Hang on a minute ... since the name derives from 'wheat' which was presumably grown around here, and 'homestead', where did that P come from anyway? And talking of wheat, is it time we came up with a gluten-free alternative?

NB The name of the Welsh village of Trellec can be spelt at least 26 ways, including Trylec, Tryleg, Trylleck. They have five different spellings in use on road signs and shops. We have to try harder!

By the way, which do you say?
weet-HAMP-sted
WEET'm'sted
HWEET-HAMP-sted
WEE-tee (WEE-tee? Really?)
WEE-toe (!!!????)
or something else entirely?

What's in a name?

W H E A T H A M P S T E A D

The name of the village is excellent for playing the game 'how many words can you make from the letters of … W H E A T H A M P S T E A D?'

• Start by finding words which are already visible with adjacent letters in the right order: WHEAT, HEATH, AT …

• Then find words with the letters in the right order – although they may be separated from one another: WHAT, MEAD, MAD …

• After which you can just go crazy and make any old word from the letters: DAMP, TEAM, PAW …

The rules (unless you're a complete maverick, or a rule obsessive) are: all words of one or more letters are acceptable, including plurals and abbreviations, but not including proper names (unless it is your own – which should keep SAM, PAM, PAT, PETE and ED happy). You can only use a letter more than once if it appears more than once in the word (eg you can use A three times) – unless you really, really need another one to make a really, really good word.

(You should definitely keep the 'p' for this game.)

With games like this, those long Wheathampstead winter evenings just fly by!

(Oh no! The plaques are all in order except two! Note to self – remember to change them)

Look out for the green plaque

The Wheathampstead Heritage Trail is an excellent guide to some of the more historic sites in the village. You can find the route on the information boards, on leaflets* or just look out for the 21 green plaques – on which you will find the answers to these questions. Get out there and follow the trail.

1. What essential bit of village equipment was kept in The Bull after 1866?
2. Who is the author of *The Compleat Angler*?
3. Bricks from which three centuries are part of the Tudor Archway?
4. Which two prime ministers owned Place Farm in the 19th century?
5. When was the station closed?
6. What were the birth and death years of the 10th Earl of Cavan?
7. What's the derivation of the surname 'Pargeter'?
8. Who was Wheathampstead Mill originally owned by?
9. What's another name for crinkle-crankle walls?
10. What colour were the trout the dignitaries fished for?
11. Who is St Helen's Church named after?
12. Who was the 'hero of Hill 60' in WWI?
13. How many years did the Old Church School remain open?
14. What was the previous name of the Hope Brewery?
15. When did the antiques business close?
16. What else was the timber-framed Swan Inn made with?
17. Who owned the Hope Brewery in the 18th century?
18. Why did Henry Sibley rebuild the frontage of his house in 1763?
19. Why has Jessamine Cottage got a lock-up? Where is it?
20. What were James Westwood's four jobs?
21. Who presented the Devil's Dyke? To whom? And to commemorate what?
22. What does the 22nd plaque commemorate? Where is it?

By the way, if you find green plaque, it's probably time to clean your teeth.

*from the post office, local shops, the Parish Council offices (at The Memorial Hall on Marford Road), or possibly in the telephone box

Mountains and molehills

Wheathampstead is pretty hilly. And just as Rome* is known as the 'city of the seven hills', we sometimes like to refer to our village as 'the Rome of Herts'. More accurately though (even if less felicitously), we should be calling it the 'village of the three (or four?) hills, two mounts, a vale and a dyke'.

The Hill is clearly making a mountain out of a molehill (but see how mountainous the village becomes if you're on a bike or pushing a buggy).

Talking of molehills, if you walk down near the river, you'll see evidence of moles popping up everywhere.
But beware. Some people have been taking the earth from molehills to use in their gardens. If you're one of them, be very careful to sieve the earth to remove mole eggs – otherwise you'll just be taking the problem home with you.

*and Lisbon, and Istanbul

More worrying than molehills and conflicted hills is that if you get a bit disorientated, the village has a tendency to disappear altogether. As a tourist official once remarked 'It's not open every day. It's only visible at weekends'. Which leaves things a little flat and puts talk of mountains into perspective.

Gently down the river

Our river flows from Luton to London for about 98 kilometres (58 miles in old money). Like the village, it isn't sure how to spell itself.
In earlier times it has been **Lig(e)an, Lygan, Luye** and **Leye**, probably coming from a Celtic word meaning 'bright' or 'light'. Now it has settled to either **Lee** or **Lea**.
A **River Lea** in Cockney Rhyming Slang is a **cup of tea** – usually a bad cup of tea (so it is not recommended to use river water to make one).

Can you work out the order of the pictures from when the river enters Wheathampstead to when it leaves?

It flows in this direction
(when you're facing this way) →

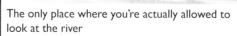

The only place where you're actually allowed to look at the river

5

Out for a duck

We're not allowed to feed the ducks any more. Bread's bad for them (and don't say 'Let them eat cake' because that's worse) and it turns out we were mainly feeding the rats! So ducks are much less likely to come swimming down the river to greet us these days. On the other hand, they've taken to foraging for themselves so you often see them hanging out round the village. And they've always preferred people's gardens as the setting for all aspects of family life – from conception to fledging.

Don't eat that!
Bread's not good for you.

Cafés usually put out duck bowls

We've got some interesting varieties.

This lady laid one egg per day for 17 days, then sat on them for 28 days. They all hatched within 24 hours of each other. (When the egg first cracks, it's called 'pipping'.) Under her wings, they were invisible.

One-legged duck?

Black headless ducks?

Not sure what these chaps were up to –
but they were a bit peeved about being caught on camera

How come Harpenden gets a sign? Surely we deserve one more than they do!

A low flying duck? You have to go to the Crooked Chimney to see 'duck or grouse'

Swanning about

Despite the rumour, not all swans belong to the queen. But she does like ours the best. Swans mate for life, so if their partner dies, they stay alone. This happened to 'lonesome George'. However he does have friends and he often hangs out with the ducks when he thinks no-one's looking.

Look cool, look cool – just keep paddling

This headless thing is catching on

... so is going walkabout

I spy ...

We like to brand everything with the Wheathampstead 'W' – even the sky. How many Ws can you spot here – and on your next walk?

Isn't this sign a bit repetitive?

If you stand on your head,
or look sideways,
you'll see a whole lot more ...

Apparently weight watchers have recently started muscling in on our W thing in a BIG way.

... something beginning with W

And then how many things beginning with W can you spot?

Is this a 'WALKing stick' or a 'walking STICK'?

Le Moulin

You'll find more on other pages of this book — and in the village. (Body parts, clothes, things in shops and branded products all count.)

Bestiary ...

How many different animals do you think you can find in the village? One beginning with every letter of the alphabet? You might like to make two lists: the animals you expect to find, and those you actually find. Meantime put these in alphabetical order and see which letters are missing – and which repeated.

If you find ants like these which are running away to get married, count them as ant-elopes

What's the plural of 'daddy-long-legs'? Daddies-long-legses?

But how close is the heron?

... it's a zoo out there

Badgers

I'm sure a quail was quailing in this bush ...

αSCALE

a kite kite

KINGFISHER CLOSE

What do you call it when worms take over the world?
ANSWER Global worming

JAGUAR

Telling the sheep from the goats

Sheep look like this
(The warning is because
they're pretty dangerous.)

Sorry! I missed taking
photographs of the lambs.
They don't hang around forever.

Follow my leader

Is everyone paying attention!?

Every animal is valued,
even if they can't all be top of the class

Apparently not!

Making a pig of yourself

Pig in the wall

If two builders start building a wall from different ends, they have to be very careful to put the same amount of mortar between the lines of bricks so that the wall remains level. If they don't ... well, try filling in the missing bricks in the wall below.

The problem you'll discover is called 'a pig in the wall'.

There's another sort of pig in the wall in the car park. And look for other semi-precious stones in the wall too.
(NB Semi-precious means they're not worth more than 50p!)

It's nice to read books about pigs – at the end there's always a twist in the tale.

Hide and seek

Some Wheathampstead animals are harder to see than others ...

Emu or ostrich?

Rather unexpectedly some large birds have moved into the village – but are they emus or ostriches?

How to tell them apart:
Ostriches are from Africa and emus from Australia (but the accents are similar).
Emus are smaller – and browner (but young ostriches are brown too – so unless they're standing next to each other ...)
Both have strong legs and can run fast – emus up to 30mph and ostriches up to 40mph (but they don't always run at full tilt).
So the clincher is the toes. Emus have three (on each foot) and ostriches two – but since they have been known to kill people with those strong legs, you really don't want to get that close.

Big Bag Wolf

If you go down to the Deep Dark Wood, be sure to go when it's bright and sunny – but still look out for the Big Bag Wolf.

Actually the wolf is very shy and tries to discourage walkers by pointing the sign away from the path. He usually hides when he hears people coming – but sometimes he leaves in such a hurry that he leaves his big bag behind. (Or is ours a she-wolf?)

- Knock knock
- *Who's there?*
- Bette
- *Bette who?*
- Bet you didn't think you'd see a zebra in Wheathampstead

The Wheathampstead zebra crossing

(never seen in daylight hours)

Every zebra has a unique 'bar code' and zebra mums walk round their newborns making sure they know their own baby. If you stroke a zebra, the black stripes stick up more than the white because the black skin is thicker. The nearer to the equator, the higher the proportion of black to white (more protection from the sun).

High spots ...

Can you identify these buildings in the High Street from their roofs? (rooves?)

14

... things are looking up

Mostly we just look at things at about head height, but we often see more if we look up (or down ... or check out just one feature such as windows or doors).

15

O ye'll tak' the high road

The High Street was named at a time when it was much higher than it is today – as you can see by looking at the height of the land on the other side of the church wall.

Is the path on the left (above) evidence of the original 'high road'?

Or this?

Wizardry

Ye olde magicke telephonie boxe is not a Tardis, but it does involve some wizardry. Look out for Harry Potter and Ron Weasley driving away as the balloons are released to celebrate the (re)instatement of the old-style red telephone box on Village Day 2014.

This is an authentic telephone box so don't expect it to work!

Wheathampstead artist Andrew Robley gets lots of Brownie points for noticing the church clock's favourite time.

These are not magic symbols. The High Street gives you the chance to start learning the world language of the future – Chinese! So, how do you pronounce these symbols? What do they mean?

17

Wheathampstead stationary

If it's a train you want, you'll wait quite a long time at Wheathampstead station. In fact, the wait is often so long that it's known to some as Wheathampstead stationary, and someone's even set up a picnic table! However you may well find a wagon waiting to be coupled to its engine and they don't mind if you jump aboard.

Platforms (plural) is a bit optimistic –
but it's well worth a visit

I ask again, how much is forty shillings!?

GBS is frequently to be seen sunning his knees (and reading the good book) in his corner at the station. Make sure you greet him politely. 'Hi George' is quite acceptable if you've encountered one another before, but that first meeting should be a bit more formal. So, do you greet him as 'Mr Shaw' or as 'Mr Bernard-Shaw'? What exactly *is* his surname?

Do ask George if, in the context of his writing, he keeps stationery. If he's in a good mood, he invariably replies, "No, sometimes I wriggle around a bit."

When is a pub not a pub?

Once upon a time Wheathampstead had 26 pubs. Today there are two in the High Street, and you can also see the spaces – both occupied and unoccupied – where a sign used to hang. You may spot similar hanging spaces around the village. But which ones are (or were) pubs?

Huge thanks to Miller & Carter for giving us back our Bull sign

Two swans? For people who **Swan Inn** and Swan Out again? (More fool them)

L'Olivo (not 'Olivio's!) previously **The Nelson** (and before that **Melbourne Arms, Horse & Jockey**)

The Bell / **The Bell & Crown** (evidence of)

Pubs or not?

The Cherry Tree – not a pub – nor as derelict as it appears

Wheathampstead or not?

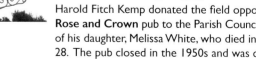

Harold Fitch Kemp donated the field opposite **The Rose and Crown** pub to the Parish Council in memory of his daughter, Melissa White, who died in 1932 aged 28. The pub closed in the 1950s and was converted into two cottages. The sign was put up in 2003.

Consult an official source if you want the real history of Wheathampstead pubs – one is due to appear soon after this book is published. While you're at it, look at Dianne Payne's book on Folly Fields for more information about Melissa White – and loads of other good stuff.

Seeing pink elephants

The name 'Elephant and Castle' could be a corruption of 'L'Infanta de Castille' (the title of a Spanish princess betrothed to King Charles I) or it could be named after the symbol of the ivory trade (an elephant with a seat on its back which looked like a castle).

More than 10,500 UK pubs have closed since 2000. Bucking the trend, The Reading Rooms opened as a micro-pub under its original name. Ironically it used to be a temperance house – an alternative gathering place for teetotallers who didn't drink alcohol. The new owners are keeping this tradition alive – browsers, chatters* and readers are all welcome. (Look out for the elephant in the room.)

The village traditionally has links with elephants, including the one who broke our quay in the 1940s (celebrated in one of Nick Schon's paintings – right), the dung of the London Zoo elephants transported by rail to Wheathampstead Station to fertilise local crops (commemorated in *The Great Wheathampstead Elephant Dung Disaster and Other Stories* by Howard Wright), our Thai Golden Elephant, and the many pink elephants which must have been seen over the years by the clientele of the 26 pubs.

Look out also for Elias (who's a bit of a white elephant) in the High Street and elsewhere, although occasionally some of the grumpier village people sprinkle elephant powder around which drives him away. In the olden days everyone used elephant powder so elephants were never seen. Most people didn't even know what they looked like, which is probably why The Elephant and Castle didn't have a pub sign – which is the case to this day.

WHEATHAMPSTEAD ELEPHANT
1940
A circus elephant damaged the Mill Quay when it came for a drink

* If you're planning to chat, you might like to check out the origin of the word which is possibly to do with chewing a hallucinogenic root (khat or qat), or could derive from an old word meaning lice – so chatting is what soldiers did in the trenches in WWI while running a lit match along the seams of their uniforms to kill the lice. ('Chatty' meant a dirty, lousey person.)

The bells, the bells

The louvres in the arch next to the clock indicate that there are probably bells within – as in this case. Unusually the bells are rung from the church floor in St Helen's so everyone can be shown the ropes.

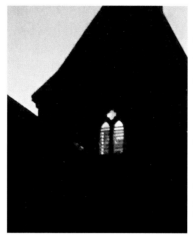

Spare a thought for the Campbell and Bellamy families who, between them, ring all day and every day, on the hour every hour.
A third family, the Clappers left years ago (giving rise to the expression 'go like the Clappers').
Mr Nobell failed at interview.
The families wish it to be known that they are bell-ringers and not campanologists.
As young Sally (named after the fluffy coloured bit of the bell rope) likes to say,
'We don't study them, we ring them!'

By the way, is ringing the only profession where you're working most effectively when you're on strike?

As Rupert Brooke so accurately noted in his famous poem *The Vicarage*, like all church clocks, ours faithfully marks the time of 'ten to three' twice in every 24-hour period at approximately the same times each day.
You'll note that like many clocks on public buildings, this one uses Roman numerals. Can you put these in order? Check whether you're correct by looking at the clock.
Then notice that one of them is different on this clock – and on most clocks.

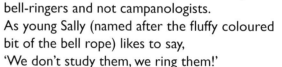

VIII   IV   XII   I   X   II   XI   V   III   VI   IX   VII

You'll see Roman numerals in a couple of places in the village. To read them, add up letters from left to right, starting with the highest.
M=1000; **D**=500; **C**=100 (think 'century'); **L**=50; **X**=10; **V**=5; **I**=1
So **MDCLXVI** is 1666 (1000+500+100+50+10+5+1)
You might find up to three of the same letter (MMM=3000) but a smaller number in front of a bigger is taken away from the bigger number:
CM=900, **CD**=400, **XC**=90, **VC**=95, **XL**=40, **IX**=9, **IV**=4
So what date was the house on the right built?

MCMLXI

ANSWER 1961=1+10+50+900+1000
Hmm – there wasn't much point in putting that answer upside down

Get me to the church on time

Two of the gargoyles on St Helen's Church are representations of people who still live in the village: Canon Tom Purchas (a previous Rector) and Colin Hazelwood (who was Chair of the church Fabric Committee). Can you tell which is which?*
Can you find them on the church? How many other gargoyles can you find?

The gargoyles were commissioned and paid for by architect Bruno Hooker in the 1980s to celebrate the work on the church, including the spire and this gargoyle window.

* The ones at the top are the gargoyles

The sword in the ~~stone~~ *tree*

If you find Wheathampstead's own Excalibur, beware the (quite) old saying:
The one who pulls the sword from the tree
Shall ne'er be the chair of the PCC

What's this?

a) window through which lepers can receive communion without coming into contact with the congregation?

b) window to look through and see the consecrated host when the church is closed?

c) medieval cat flap (cats being employed to keep down the poor church mice)

d) none of the above
   (what's your suggestion?)

The dead centre of Wheathampstead

There are lots of interesting things to find in St Helen's churchyard. Our **Angel of Wheathampstead** is less famous than Antony Gormley's **Angel of the North**, but although the northern angel is much, much wider, as you can see, the two are exactly the same height – and ours is clearly taller if you count the cross.

How's your Latin?

What does this mean? ...

REQUIESCAT IN PACE

and this (*in cruce spero*)?

in cruce spero

and (from the RC church) these initials?

A skull is a typical example of the Latin phrase *memento mori*, which means 'reminder of death'. These two examples are in – or outside – St Helen's Church. The picture below shows some of the children of Sir John and Elizabeth Garrard. How many did they have? And how many of those died young (they're holding skulls)?

James Marshall's tombstone explains how in his will of 1719 he bequeathed his estate to the churchwardens of St Helen's for '*the purpose of putting out poor men's children ... to some trade*'. Three hundred years later, the James Marshall Foundation still gives grants to young people in Wheathampstead and Harpenden for costs related to education, training or work opportunities which are beyond their resources.

What's the link between these two memorials?

Are the railings around this tomb to keep people out? Or to keep someone or something in?

Getting cross

As you discover the interesting and beautiful tombstones, younger members can be looking for the many different crosses (while practising numbers and maths, and looking for examples of the letter W). For a start, can you find all of these?

Sanctum sanctorum

Everyone is welcome to enter St Helen's church – and see how many of these you can spot. (If you're a regular church goer, can you identify them before you look?)

In
memory of Lilian
Sybil Keen 1903-1970
benefactor of this Church
and her brother Maunsell
Edward Normington
George 1905-1976
formerly of this
parish

IN THANKS TO GOD
FOR THE LIFE OF

PATRICK OGDEN
1932-1968

WHOSE VISION
AND ENTERPRISE
CONTRIBUTED
SO MUCH TO THE
PLANNING & BUILDING
OF THIS ORGAN

DIRECTLY VNDERNEATH THIS PLACE, LYETH BVRIED
IOHN HEYWORTH OF MACKEYRE END ESQVIER &
IOANE HIS WIFE, THEY HAD 3 CHILDREN BVRYED IN
THERE INFANCIE, WHERE FORE THEY BOOTH DID

I am you are the branches VINE

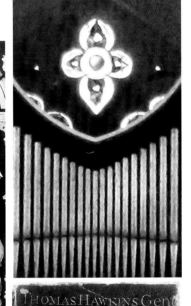

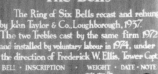

The Bells

The Ring of Six Bells recast and rehung by John Taylor & Co., Loughborough, 1957. The two Trebles cast by the same firm 1972 and installed by voluntary labour in 1974, under the direction of Frederick W. Ellis, Tower Capt.

BELL	INSCRIPTION	WEIGHT cwts qtrs lbs	DATE	NOTE
Treble	GIVEN BY THE Bellringers	3·2·13	1972	
2ND	GIVEN BY Wm. John Tame	4·0·11		
3RD		4·2·2	1957	
4TH		5·0·4	"	C
5TH		6·0·22	"	B♭
6TH		7·1·4	"	A
7TH		9·1·21	"	G
Tenor		14·0·22		F

On the bell board in the church are three letters which are missing in this picture. What word do they spell?

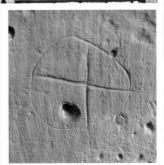

THOMAS HAWKINS Gent died the 26 Jan. 1804 Aged 83.

JANE SIBLEY Died Dec.r 21st 1826. Aged 87 Years.

And of her Sister SOPHIA SIBLEY, died Dec.r 3rd 1844, Aged 9

You'll also find pictures from inside the church on several other pages (which ones?)

Going postal

Like many things in Wheathampstead, all the postboxes in the village manage to be different.
Postboxes were introduced in early Victorian times shortly after Rowland Hill started the Penny Post in 1840.
At first they were green (like Santa Claus – until Coca Cola got involved as an advertising gimmick), but by about 1879 they had all been painted pillar box red. (Wasn't the name a lucky coincidence?)

Unique – no slot for letters!

Have you ever seen one like this anywhere else?

Notice the optimistic time of the next collection

By the way ... the first stamp ever issued was the Penny Black, and because stamps were invented in the UK, Britain is the only country in the world which does not write its name on postage stamps – as long as they bear the image of the monarch.

Blackmore End has this George VI box

Pretty but don't post letters here

Every postbox bears the Royal Cypher: the initials of the monarch who was reigning when it was installed.
The **R** stands for **Rex** (king) or **Regina** (queen) in Latin.
V is for **Victoria** (we have a Victorian pillar box in the village).
G stands for **George**, and **E** for **Edward** or **Elizabeth**.
The Roman numeral tells you which ... **GVR** (George the fifth), **GVIR**, **EVIIR, EVIIIR** and our own dear queen **EIIR**. (See Roman numerals page 22)
So which monarch is it if you only see **GR**?
And why won't you find **EIR**?*

* I GR must be George the fifth – because that was the only option at the time. The postal system was not invented until long after the reigns of both Elizabeth I and Edward I

Odd schools

Which is the
odd-one-out?*

* St Helen's is the only existing church school. St Albans High School for Girls is the only one all girls school. Aldwickbury, all boys and not in Wheathampstead. The National School (later the Old Church School) is not a school. It's the only one now used as offices. The existence of the old (the only) secondary school is only hinted at in a street name. So the answer is Beech Hyde – the only one which is the odd-one-out because it isn't the odd-one-out for any other reason.

Looking round

You may not find these exact same examples – but once you start looking, it's hard not to see round things. (By the way, what are they all?)

Apart from the obvious, can you find: wastebin, beer mat, coffee cup, sugar jar, beer keg, drain cover x2, chair, table, tree trunk, watering can, bottle top, plant pot, car wheel, car light, wall light, window, Manor pharmacy symbol, glass ornament, window pattern x3, symbols in church x2, reflector on gate, hanging plant ball, scooter wheel, GBS's button, side table, belisha beacon, apple on tree, bollard, street lamp (from below), extractor fan x2, button on dress, letter O on signs x3, traffic light (green), door furniture x4, coil of wire, Christmas bauble (why?), end of wall strengthener x2, car petrol cover, parts of graves x2, gym equipment knob, green stud on bench, red thing at station, signs on buildings x2, war memorial, knobbles on pavement, sticker, thing I can't remember x2, the photographer x2

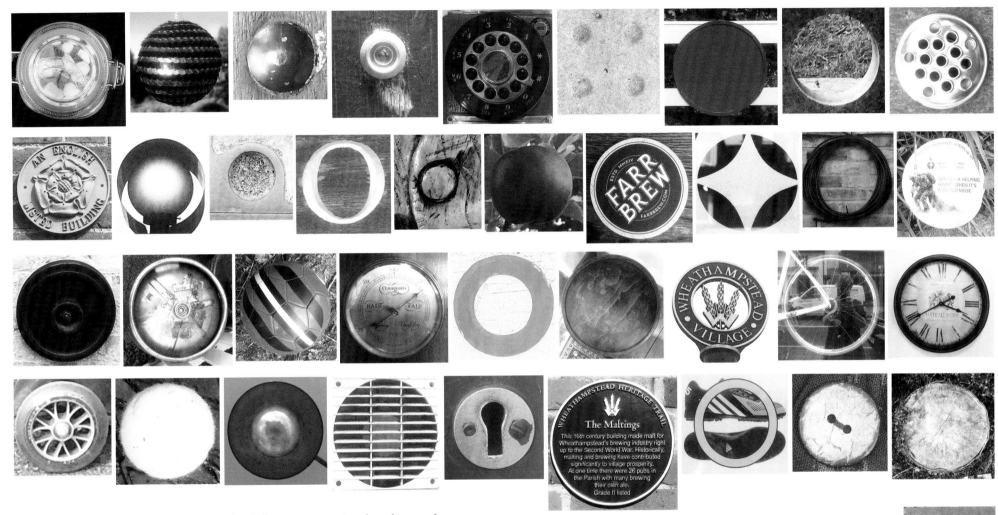

When you (finally) run out of circles, look for squares, triangles, diamonds, stars ...

... and you never know where you'll find the heart of the village

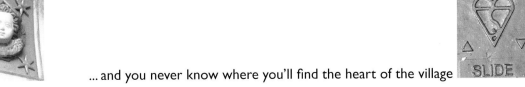

Inspiring Wheathampstead

Which three (plus one*) of these spires are in Wheathampstead? (By the way, where in the village can you find 'inspiring women'?**)

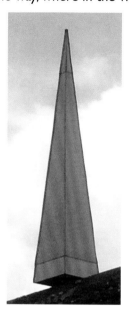

* The 'plus one' is St Peter's Church in Gustard Wood

** If you don't know, ask someone in the Women's Institute

Crinkle-crankle walls

We're very proud of our crinkly-crankly walls. But which ones are crinkles and which are crankles? How many of each are there?

If you drew the wall from above, would it look like this...?

...or like this?

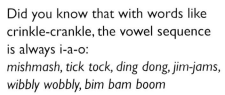

Did you know that with words like crinkle-crankle, the vowel sequence is always i-a-o:
mishmash, tick tock, ding dong, jim-jams, wibbly wobbly, bim bam boom

Look out too for the secret garden

It's a dog's life

Look at these pictures again carefully. What do you notice? That's right — no cats!
There are loads of dogs in Wheathampstead, but almost no cats. So you get one point for every dog you see, but 10 points for a cat.

Sorry – I missed a couple of the most important dogs in the village, so here are frames for you to draw or stick in photos of special dogs of your acquaintance. (Or cats, if you must.)

35

Famous Wheathampsteadonions

Match the labels with the pictures of these famous people associated with Wheathampstead. Which ones can you find on other pages of this book? Look for more evidence of them in the village – particularly in street names and signs.

ABBOT JOHN
Two times Abbot of St Albans Abbey
Rescued and healed King Henry VI

DAME ELLEN TERRY
Stage and screen actress

JOHN BUNYAN
17th century author and preacher

LADY CAROLINE LAMB
British aristocrat and novelist renowned for her affair with Lord Byron. Lived in Brocket Hall

CAPTAIN GEORGE UPTON ROBINS
Won the King's Medal
Killed in action Neuve Chapelle 1915

CASSIVELLAUNUS
British Chieftain warrior who led the defence against Julius Caesar

GEOFFREY DE HAVILLAND
Aviation pioneer and engineer

GRAHAM DANGERFIELD
Naturalist, broadcaster and zoo owner

APSLEY CHERRY-GARRARD
Antarctic explorer with Capt Scott's last expedition, and owner of Lamer Park

THE WICKED LADY
Highwaywoman

GEORGE BERNARD SHAW
Playwright and social thinker

By the way, can you find the swan? There's one in every picture.

LOCALS, BY LOCALS, FOR THE LOCAL

A Community Project organised by St Helen's Church

These pictures (the brainchild of Richard Banham, Rector of St Helen's) were drawn by Wheathampstead artist Nick Schon (who's illustrated most of the Biff and Chip reading books). They were transferred to boards which were painted by local people and put up around The Swan pub in 2013 while it was out of action after a fire. After being stored for five years, some of them can now be seen on a garage near the crinkle-crankle wall, on the map boards in East Lane, on cards – and in this book.

Wheat'mstdonions in the making

RUDOLPH LAMBART
EARL OF CAVAN 1865-1946
Fought in the Boer War and WW1

LORD BROCKET
Ferrari enthusiast

WILLIAM BEECH THOMAS
1868-1952
Decorated WW1 correspondent
and enthusiast for village life and
countryside matters

Reginald Owen
1887-1972
Actor
Made 145 films including
Mary Poppins

SARAH CHURCHILL
DUCHESS OF MARLBOROUGH
1660-1744
Companion of Queen Anne and one of
the richest women in Europe

Wheathampsteadonions

The old folk

The current population of Wheathampstead is so old that there are even warning signs ...

And when I say old, I'm not kidding.

The council have tried to fight back by restricting the village centre to young people under 20 ...

But the old folk don't give up that easily and not all the youngsters survive ...
Look out for the memorials on the road to those who didn't make it

Disgusted of Wheathampstead

We in Wheathampstead pride ourselves on our education, and we're usually very fastidious about grammar, punctuation and the like (for example, when we talk about William Shakespeare in the past tense, we refer to him as Wouldiwas Shookspeared). So, many people wrote variations on this letter about the two notices below:

Dear Sir or Madam

You are clearly unaware of the rules concerning the use of full stops in abbreviations. If the final letter of the full word is used, no full stop is needed. If the word is 'interrupted', then use a full stop. (Some modernists leave them out altogether, but I have no truck with them!)

St Helen does not need or want one. (And don't claim that it's the abbreviation for 'street' because it clearly isn't, although I admit that 'St' for 'Street' can be argued either way.)

But the absolute horror is your use – or not – of apostrophes. HELEN'S needs the apostrophe whether you are saying she is near, or (presumably) that this section of road is named after her.

Similarly, although your yellow sign may sometimes describe the situation when residents are actually parking here, you clearly meant to indicate that this is a place where one or more residents may park. The sign should read RESIDENTS' PARKING, or at a push, if its a small space, RESIDENT'S PARKING.

It's grammar is just wrong!

I remain, yours faithfully

Disgusted of Wheathampstead

Shortly after writing this particular letter, of course, the author had to leave the village in shame and ignominy, having become a laughing stock.*

No-one really knows why the windows of this house were bricked up. Possibly it was to avoid paying the C18th-19th window tax – but since the door is also blocked, locals whisper that 'Disgusted' is holed up here, never actually having left the village. Mothers use her as a threat when their children are misbehaving. Her house in Rong Wroad – just around the corner from Wright Close – remains empty.

*Why did she become a laughing stock?

High and mighty

There are some exceptionally tall people in the village, so we have to set height restrictions in certain areas...

although there are also very short people.

Some of the non-average people choose to live together – and are not shy about being different.

The story goes that (like the one in Amsterdam) this house was built by a nobleman for his servant after hearing him say "I would be happy to have a house as wide as your front door." Unfortunately it later caught fire and developed a list to rival the famous tower in Pisa. If only there were someone in the village qualified to prop it up!*

There is much evidence in the village of the warring nature of the inhabitants.

People are proud to show their allegiance ...

and their achievements

although some prefer just to watch

and military types all use their titles

Children are encouraged to start young

DEVIL'S DYKE
Battle between Cassivelaunus (Celt) and Julius Caesar (Roman)

But of course, like every village, we also have some perfectly lovely people to keep us all sane.

*There is. The man responsible for stopping the leaning tower of Pisa from leaning any further, is engineer and long-time resident of Wheathampstead, John Burland.

41

What on earth...?

Iron age settlement? Relatives of the Easter Island statues? Rival to stonehenge?
The evidence of aliens we've been searching for?
The only thing we're fairly confident of is that they are in pairs – maybe male/female?
Can you exercise your brain as you work out which ones pair up?

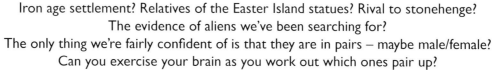

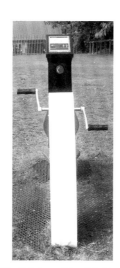

Archeologists have recently discovered their names: Bud, Dud, Deibi, Larakin, Melia and Desperado. Which is which? (Or can you think of better names?)

Somewhere ...

Look for colours – one colour at a time.

Then look at something red (around the village – or the Titmuss wagon on page19) and see how it isn't one colour at all. It's also orange, or pink, white in the light, purple in the shade ...Try it with blue, green, yellow and other colours too.

Also rans

Just a few final things to look for. No help, except to say that they're all fairly central in the village.

Shouldn't this picture be on the dog page? What's a dentil?

What's with the disembodied arms?

DIY – over to you

After a book full of daft explanations for things, if it pleases you, make up stories of your own for these final, final pictures.

Answers and stuff

① Whelcome to Wheathampstead

12d (pence)=1 shilling; 20 shillings=£1; 40 shillings=£2
Even if that notice was from 1970 (and it's probably much older), in today's money £1 would be worth more than £15 (so a 40 shilling fine would cost you at least £30)
1 pole = 25.3m². Go online and find out about rods, roods and perches too.
I couldn't find anyone to confirm that we are (or are not) trying to contact aliens – not officially anyway.

②¼ Give us a sign

The sign coming into the village from St Albans down The Hill is not so much missing as lost in the fog.

③ What's in a name?

Type 1: A, WE, HE, HEAT, EAT, HAM, HAD, AM, AMP, MP, TEA, AD
Type 2: HAT, (HATH & HAST if you're old fashioned), ATE, APE, ED, HATE, DATE, SAD, PAD, WAD, WET, TAD, SEA, MEAD, TAMP, HEAD, PEA, EAST, WEST, WED, WEE (meaning 'little' obviously), WEED, HEAP, THAT, WHAM
Others: AWE, DEATH(S), DEEM(S), DEEP, DESERT, DESSERT (= anagram of STRESSED so really really good word), DETEST, DEW, HADES (doesn't count, proper name), MADE, MAST, MATE(S), PAT(S), PATE, PATH(S), PEAT, PEST, SAME, SAT, SAW, SEAT, SEE, SET, STAMP, STEM, TEAM(S), TEASE, TEAT(S), TEE(S), TEST, TESTED, WADE(S), WHET(S) … and more.

③¼ To P or not to P Please say you noticed the 'keeping the peace' pun.

④ Gently down the river

Did you spot the **spiling**? The woven fences of willow branches which hold up the river bank and encourage people to enter the river at designated points. The clever thing is that the willow sprouts roots into the bank and starts growing, so with time the support gets stronger.

⑯ O ye'll tak' the high road

The real reason the churchyard is higher than the road – and the reason many churches look as if they're sinking – is the thousands of burials which have taken place in the graveyard over the years.

⑰ Wizardry

The symbols are pronounced **Ni hau** – which means **Hello**
(literally **You good?**)

③ Look out for the green plaque

These are written extra small because you're supposed to go out and look at the plaques. I genuinely had fun finding them – and actually learnt quite a lot of stuff (just enough). 1 The Bull – Its fire engine • 2 River Lea – Izaak Walton • 3 Tudor archway – C16th, 18th & 19th • 4 Wheathampstead Place – Lord Melbourne & Lord Palmerston • 5 Station – 1965 • 6 Wheathampstead House – 1865-1946 • 7 The surname Pargeter comes from 'pargeting', the type of plasterwork decoration you can see on The Old Bakery • 8 Wheathampstead Mill – originally owned by Westminster Abbey • 9 Crinkle-crankle walls – Serpentine walls • 10 Bury Farm Cottages – Pink trout • 11 St Helen's Church – The Roman Empress Helena (She was the mother of the Emperor Constantine I, and she apparently discovered Christ's cross and was made a saint, but it doesn't say this bit on the plaque) • 12 Churchyard – Captain George Upton Robins (one of the Wheathampsteadonions on page 37) • 13 Old Church School – 107 years, from 1862 to 1969 (And zig-zag is another of those i-a-o words like crinkle-crankle, but do you spell zigzag with or without a hyphen?) • 14 Brewhouse & Maltings – Originally the Parrott Brewery • 15 Collins Corner – 2006 (Since then the building has been a restaurant – currently Oxscale) • 16 The Swan Inn – Wattle and daub (Extra info: wattle is a woven lattice of wooden strips which are 'daubed' with a sticky material usually made of some combination of straw, wet soil, clay, sand – and animal dung! Yum!) • 17 Lattimores – The Lattimore family (obviously) • 18 The White Cottage – As a present for his second wife • 19 Jessamine Cottage – It has a lock-up under the stairs because it used to be a police house • 20 The Two Brewers – innkeeper, blacksmith, bell ringer and village fireman • 21 The Devils' Dyke was presented to no one in particular… well, look at the plaque (right) • There is a 22nd plaque – there's a (small) picure of it somewhere in this book – and it's not mentioned on the heritage boards (yet) … but keep an eye open next time you go for a Thai meal.

THE DEVILS DYKE
WAS PRESENTED BY
THE RT HON LORD BROCKET
TO COMMEMORATE
THE CORONATION OF
THEIR MAJESTIES
KING GEORGE VI
AND
QUEEN ELIZABETH
13 MAY 1937

⑧ I spy … something beginning with W

wagon • waist • walking stick • weir • waste bin • water • watering can • watermelon • web • WC (& wall) • weathervane • weed • wheatsheaf • weeping willow / willow • windscreen / wipers • wrist • wheelchair (symbol) • wrapping paper • wheel • window • windowsill • wheelbarrow • watch • windmill (= Le Moulin in French) • but Why is the Y here?
Others in the book: wasp • woman • wood • worm • words • writing • wine • wing • wires • wolf (evidence of) • wizard (Others to look for in the village: wallet • waistcoat • walker • washing powder • Weetabix • wellingtons • whiskers • whisky • washing-up liquid • whistle …)
And if you're prepared to mispronounce 'r's, you've got westauwant, woad, wectowy, etc.

When I explained about Ws, my grandson did this. I choose to think he was being helpful.

How many W-things can you do while you're looking for W-things? whistle, wink, wait, wilt, wobble, wiggle, wriggle, witter, wimper, whine, wail, weep, wheeze, wave, wobble, waffle, wade, wage war, wrangle, wound, wander, wonder…

Once you've done W, you've got 25 other letters to explore.

⑩ Bestiary … it's a zoo out there

Animals elsewhere in the book are in **bold**: ant (antelope) • badgers • bee • (bird) • blackbird • blue tit • bull • butterfly • chicken/chicks • cockerel • cows • daddy-long-legs • (no dog, it's crossed out) • **dogs** • deer • dragonfly • duck • **ducklings** • elephant • **emu** (or ostrich?) • flamingo • fish (& symbol) • giraffes • goose/geese • goat/ram • **goats** • heron (close) • horse (& horsehead) • jaguar • kingfisher (close) • kite • ladybird (US ladybug) • lamb • leopard(cheetah?) • lion x2 • **moles** (evidence of) • monkey • moorhen • moose • **ostrich** (or emu?) • octopus • owl x2 • ox(scale) • **pig** • pigeon • quail (in bush?) • ram/goat • robin • seagull • sheep(cote lane) • snail • spider • starfish • **swans** • tiger • toad • unicorn • wasp • **wolf** (evidence of) • worm • **zebra**

㉒ The bells, the bells

There are no bell families – the hour is struck mechanically by a hammer on the outside of the bell. However St Helen's does have a band of bell ringers who ring before the 9.30 service and on special occasions. Learners (and returners) welcome.

㉓ Get me to the church on time

• Tom Purchas' gargoyle is right. Colin Hazlewood is the one that's left. Their photos are the other way round. The carving was done by a stone mason not a sculptor so you probably wouldn't identify them in a line-up – but you can tell the gargoyles apart by the hairline.
• The door is called a 'beggar's squint' or 'leper's squint', or a 'hagioscope' (which means to look – scope – at something sanctified – hagio). So I'm not sure what its primary purpose was but it probably isn't (c) so you're welcome to make up your own purpose.

26 Sanctum sanctorum

The title is Latin for 'holy of holies' – or possibly 'hiding place (sanctuary) of the saints'.
Most of the floor tiles are Victorian, but the ones near the altar are 'encaustic Maw' tiles (made by the family of Nonwy Maw) and the old broken ones around the font are medieval (very old). The font appears twice more: the bluey-green cover, and a decorative carving of a leopard (or lion?). The original (very old) font was apparently taken to St Nicholas' Church in Harpenden and we're still a bit cross about it.
Ford Bath was a sculptor – 'ft' stands for Latin 'fecit' meaning 'made (by)'.
Two of the stained glass windows show (unusually) (a) Jesus doing carpentry with Joseph and (b) Mary weaving. (Nice to think of them as an ordinary family doing ordinary things. Look out too for Jesus preaching in the temple as a boy.)
The fragments in the Lamer Chapel window are from the large (now plain glass) window which was destroyed by a bomb (some people were quite pleased because now there is more light). The empty spaces below the fragment window would probably once have housed small statues – although the right-hand carving is unfinished, so maybe there were none.
If the carved face on the niche in the Lady Chapel has leaves around it, it may represent the pagan Green Man aka Jack o' the Green – pagan oo-er!
There are two pictures from the tomb of Sir John Brocket, one the face of his wife Margaret, the other a side panel made of alabaster showing a token number of their 10 sons (their three daughters are on the opposite side).
The very old graffiti is on a pillar near the choir stalls at the back of the church. There is more old graffiti in the crossing.
The letters missing from the bell board picture are FED. The bells are tuned to these notes – in the key of F major.
The last picture – of the beautiful coloured ceiling – is a bit surprising because the letters seem to be 'ihr'. It might stand for 'Iesus hominum redemptor' (Jesus redeemer of men). But one would expect the more common 'ihs' – the first three letters of 'Jesus' in Greek (also known as a Christogram) – which you will find on tombstones. For additional sensible and interesting information please see Ruth Jeavons' book, available in the church, *St Helen's Church – a brief history and guide*.

42 What on earth...?

This picture might help you match up the fronts and backs if you use it as an alternative to the one bottom left.

44 Also rans

The brick pattern is known as 'dentil' or 'dog's tooth'. It's on the arch nearly opposite the post office (and opposite the stylised 'O' on page 44), and you'll find the indent in the wall just round the corner going into Mount Road.
The disembodied arms are a heraldic device which appear twice on the Garrard Memorial in St Helen's Church – they are part of the Barkham family crest and they are holding a sheath of arrows (see pic at top of page).
The other things are: up high on Station Road; up high just into East Lane – possibly linked (despite the difference in spelling) to Riverdale House on the High Street which must back on to it; on Marford Road next to the fire station; two more are up high – and one down low – on the Tesco side of the High Street; next to the telephone box on the other side of the High Street; up high on the green between the crinkle-crankle walls and Ash Grove.

The Garrard Memorial

32 Inspiring Wheathampstead

Inspiring Women is the slogan of the Women's Institute – with our three separate groups, we have three times as many inspiring women as most villages.

For the rest, please go online to find out more about whatever interests you – and go out into the village to find more whonders.

24 The dead centre of Wheathampstead

The actual height of the Angel of the North is 20m.
The memorial inside the church is to Apsley Cherry-Goddard – the explorer who returned safely from Scott's expedition to the antarctic. (Was that the north or south pole?) He's also one of the page 37 pics. The memorial outside the church – an example of a Celtic cross – honours George Benet Cherry-Goddard (his father, I think). (By the way, the Celtic cross appears to predate Christianity by at least 3000 years.)
The Garrards had 14 children, two of whom died young. (Is Elizabeth – Mrs Garrard – holding her legs up in a yoga pose? Quite a feat for all eternity!)
RIP stands both for the Latin *Requiescat In Pace*, and for the English translation *Rest In Peace*.
In cruce spero means 'In the cross I hope'
INRI stands for 'Jesus of Nazareth King of the Jews' – the words written on the cross by the Romans.
I=J and Rex=King in Latin (you know that – see page 28)
NB *Pro patria* on the war memorial means 'for country'.

40 Disgusted of Wheathampstead

its (no apostrophe)=belonging to it
it's=*it is* or *it has*
She should have written: ... if it's a small space
... Its grammar is just wrong!

In Ireland we discovered that their postboxes are still green – and that this is where our river comes for a holiday.

How observant are you?

How many of these questions can you answer without looking back at the book?

1. Which of the 'page numbers revealed' (opposite page) is not the same as the one used on its page in the book? Is there more than one?
2. How many languages are used in this book?
3. What is the good book GBS keeps beside him?
4. How many green plaques are there in the village?
5. Two crinkle-crankle walls. Four pictures – each wall from both sides. Or not?
6. Which page title is different in the contents list? What is the full title? Why?
7. On how many pages do swans appear?
8. Which part of the statue of the crucifix (pictured here) was used in the book?
9. Which two Greek letters appear prominently in this book? Where? Why?
10. What year does the Roman numeral (pictured here – below) represent?
11. What's the link between Queen Elizabeth I and the road and fence design (below)?
12. Which King Henry did Abbot John rescue?
13. Which year is on the Melissa Field sign?
14. How many (main) colours are there in the rainbow on page 43?
15. Which is your favourite part of Wheathampstead (in the village or in the book)?
16. What else do you wish had been included?

ANSWERS

For some of the answers, all you need to do is look. For the others ... (2) Five languages: English, Latin, French, Greek and Chinese. (4) There are 22 plaques in the village but The Maltings does not appear on the public boards. (5) Not. One of the walls is photographed from slightly further along because one side of one of the walls is not accessible to the public. (6) What's the name of the nursery? (7) Three. Two swans on page 5, four on page 7, two on page 20. (8) The letters INRI, from the crucifix in the grounds of St Thomas More's Roman Catholic Church, are on page 24. (9) Alpha and Omega (from windows in St Helen's Church) are the first and last letters of the Greek alphabet and are often used to mean 'the beginning and the end' – as in this book. (10) The Roman numeral is 2012. (11) QEI is a Tudor queen. The fence design is a Tudor rose. (12) Henry VI – which number is that? (14) Six. Indigo and violet are often conflated into purple these days. (15-16) How about making your own scrapbook of the things you particularly like about Wheathampstead?

Page numbers revealed

Thanks and apologies

Thank you ...

... to the people who contributed directly to this book ...

Nick Schon for his talent and generosity in painting and donating all the fabulous Wheath'mstdonions and for the loan of his bag

Brian Gwinn, Mike Hollick and Sayling Low for the photos of the making of the Wheathampsteadonions

Katy Jaques for her artistic and technical exertise and help, and specifically for Elias the Elephant

Ruth Jeavons (History Soc whizz & Katy's mum) for the illuminating walk round St Helen's Church

'Rubbish professor' friend Carla for suggesting page 2¼ (if Harry Potter can have Platform 9¾ ...)

Joanna Corscaden for nurturing and photographing the ducklings

Bob Beale for recognising an ostrich when he sees one

Tamsin for the past tense of Shakespeare

Joanna and Alexander for spotting and snapping the Wheathamstead (sic) sign, the cat picture, the crucial last-minute comments which made all the difference – and for everything else

Jan Cisek for his ongoing design expertise and technological wizardry

And most of all Hugh, for undertaking without complaint the tedious job of sizing, lightening, improving(!) and making fit for printing all the photos, his many other contributions, for putting up with me through the gestating and birthing process, and for sharing this and everything else to make life so joyously worth living

... to all the people, paid and unpaid, who put so much time, thought and energy into keeping the village tidy, renovated and interesting, including ...

Julia Warren and the Parish Council

The WDPS (Wheathampstead and District Preservation Society)

Annie Brewster for her tireless work to improve the quality of our collective lives (to whom thanks also for her kind comments on the back of the book)

Patrick McNeill for his services to the river

Eddie Cornell for the Station Platform, footpaths, litterblitz and so much more

John Burgess (mad, bad, and extraordinarily hard working and generous with his time)

Miller & Carter for restoring our Bull pub sign – and for the other bull

The owners of the Necton Road house who share their skeleton (which has recently got down to bare bones, but has not been pictured nude to avoid an X-raying for the book)

Sarah-Fay Miller and her team for clearing up dog poo – and for the brilliant yoga signs

All the walkers, runners, scouts and ordinary folk who take the time to pick up litter

This book is about looking at things in Wheathampstead, but there is so much more going on. It's the people that really make it such a wonderful place to live. It is a privilege to be part of such a friendly, generous, warm and supportive community. Thank you.

Apologies ...

To all the people who do so much for the village but who aren't mentioned here. Please know that you are still greatly appreciated.

To all the people who were expecting a more serious book about Wheathampstead – to them I recommend ...

The forthcoming book on the pubs of Wheathampstead

Ruth Jeavons' book on (and available in) St Helen's Church

The Story of the Folly by Dianne Payne (£15 from 40 Folly Fields or by post +p&p dianne.payne14@btinternet.com)

... and you should make sure you join

The History Society (ring Ruth Jeavons on 01582 629516)

and WDPS wheathampsteadpreservation.org.uk

Sorry too to Rob Milner and the St Helen's Choir for not finding a way of capturing the fabulous singing in pictures

For all the other whonderful things I've omitted – I regretfully had to stop somewhere

For all the errors in this book – intentional and unintentional. Mea culpa, mea culpa, mea maxima culpa

This picture is an apology to Toby and Harry for the cat gag on page 34

Thanks too to the Friends of St Helens for helping maintain the historic church building for the benefit of everyone in the village. They will receive the profits from this book.

about how this book came about

The idea for this book was born some years back on yet another walk with small grandsons to count the ducks! I was impatient to get there, count ducks, pick up supper from the shop … and they stopped to delight in yet another worm. I was mid-sigh when it suddenly dawned on me what I was missing, and that the journey is as important as the destination. From that moment on I started seeing things through their eyes – looking for T for Toby or H for Harry in the cracks in the path, enjoying all the animals, and seeing that metal object in the tree as our very own Excalibur…

After my mother died, I was brought up by a very down-to-earth father with a great sense of humour. But I had to teach myself to be more creative. So each day I would get dressed in a different order (anything except pants ending up outside trousers), get to university by a different route, only look down, or up (the day I sprained my ankle), invent stories by linking any three random items, look at specific details along the way (numbers, letters, windows…) and generally challenge myself to think outside the box – or at least differently. Now I find I can't stop.

The real reason I wrote this book …
"I went outside once but the graphics were terrible."
The young person's joke would be funnier if it weren't so close to the truth, especially when there is so much for our eyes and brains to delight in … if we just take the time to look.

I remember being really impressed by a primary teacher who introduced a **Museum of Boring Things** on a table in the corner of the classroom. Children brought in anything they thought was boring, but it could only be included if nobody could think of a reason why it was interesting. The museum remained empty. And I am never bored.

Secretly I would like to be one of those walkers you see striding through Wheathampstead, flashing their sun-bronzed knees. But the reality is that although I enjoy the outdoors when I'm in it, I hate pointless walks. Counting steps doesn't do it for me, especially since I found out you were supposed to do 10,000 a day, when I'd been congratulating myself that going to the post office and back was (as I thought) my obligatory 1,000. But a diagnosis of diabetes pushed me into finding a reason for walking more, and taking the 600 odd(!) photos in this book encouraged me to look at our glorious village with new eyes, to delight in the details, to find out more about our history, to notice the oddities – and to make up stories about any or all of it. Walks now are never pointless.

ABOUT THE AUTHOR

After cutting her publishing teeth with Time Life Books (in the days of proper typesetting and galley proofs), Susan has gone on to earn a living as a freelance teacher, trainer and author. Under various noms de plume (principally Susan Norman), she has written considerably more books than JK Rowling. Early aberrations were *The History of Road Transport* and *The Behaviour of Downland Suckler Cattle* and most of the profitable ones were for foreigners learning English. More recently they have been on aspects of accelerated learning and published by Saffire Press (= Hugh and Susan). You might conceivably be interested in *Spd Rdng – the Speed Reading Bible*. This one – the first published in the name Susan L'Estrange – is for the fun of it (and for charity). Susan and Hugh moved into the village on a snowy night in 2010 to be closer grandparents – ils ne regrettent rien.

There's no place like Wheathampstead (Birdsong? Twitter? A musical tweet?)

*"To see a world in a grain of sand
and a heaven in a wild flower"*

William Blake　Auguries of Innocence
actually the whole poem is worth (re)visiting

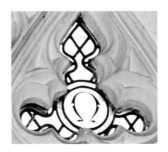